Nomads of the Sahara

WARREN J. HALLIBURTON

EDITED BY
KATHILYN SOLOMON PROBOSZ

CRESTWOOD HOUSE
NEW YORK

MAXWELL MACMILLAN CANADA
TORONTO

MAXWELL MACMILLAN INTERNATIONAL
NEW YORK OXFORD SINGAPORE SYDNEY

ACKNOWLEDGMENTS

The editor would like to acknowledge the help of Lee Morgan, whose generosity and willingness to share insights and information were invaluable in the creation of this book.

All photos courtesy of Magnum Photos.

Special thanks to Laura Straus for her assistance in putting this project together.

PHOTO CREDITS: COVER: *Arthur Tress*; *Marc Riboud* 4, 6, 21, 41, 43; *Abbas* 8, 23; *Steve McCurry* 10, 13, 31, 44, 46; *Bruno Barbey* 14; *Thomas Hoepker* 16; *George Rodger* 19, 29, 36, 38; *Susan Meiselas* 25; *Arthur Tress* 26; *Ian Berry* 32; *Dennis Stock* 34

Cover design, text design and production: William E. Frost Associates Ltd.

Library of Congress Cataloging-in-Publication Data

Halliburton, Warren J.
    The nomads of the Sahara / by Warren Halliburton;
edited by Kathilyn Solomon Probosz. — 1st ed.
p. cm. — (Africa today)
    Summary: Describes the history, culture, and daily life of the four nomadic groups that make their homes in the Sahara Desert.
    ISBN 0-89686-678-5
    1. Nomads — Sahara — Juvenile literature. [1. Nomads — Sahara.
2. Sahara — Social life and customs.] I. Probosz, Kathilyn Solomon.
II. Title. III. Series: Africa today
GN651.H35 1992
966'.008'69 — dc20   91-47153

CRESTWOOD HOUSE   MAXWELL MACMILLAN CANADA, INC.
MACMILLAN PUBLISHING COMPANY   1200 Eglinton Avenue East
866 Third Avenue   Suite 200
New York, NY 10022   Don Mills, Ontario M3C 3N1

Macmillan Publishing Company is part of the Maxwell Communication Group of Companies.
First edition
Printed in the United States of America

1   2   3   4   5   6   7   8   9   10

Contents

NOTE: The images in this book are meant to convey visually the spirit of life in the Sahara Desert, and are therefore not captioned. For full descriptions of the photos *see page 45*.

Introduction

The sun has not yet risen in the Sahara Desert. Yet the people are awake. Three cloaked figures sit beside the orange-red embers of a campfire, their backs turned against the harsh winds. Dark blue turbans wrapped around their faces protect them from the waves of sand that blow across the desert. Only their eyes are visible. They are the leaders of the People of the Veil, the Tuaregs.

The Tuaregs are the largest of the four groups of **nomads** that live in the Sahara Desert, which also include the Fulani, Moors and Arabic nomads. In Arabic, Tuareg means "abandoned by God." They are followers of Islam, the Muslim religion, but they are not Arabic. They live in Africa, but they are not black Africans. Some say they are descended from the Berbers, people who lived in North Africa over three thousand years ago. Others believe they came from Libya. Like the faces they hide behind their veils, the Tuaregs' origins are shrouded in mystery.

Beyond the elders, in the sand-swept darkness, the 20 families that make up this clan break camp. The sheep did not provide enough milk yesterday, and the elders are worried. Sheep need to eat grass to make milk, so the fact that they have not produced means that the grasses in this area are almost wiped out. The clan must move on.

The women pack the camel-skin tents, blankets and food. The girls pack the *calabashes*, bowls made from dried gourds, into leather saddlebags and make sure the *guerbas*, goatskins filled with water, are covered tightly.

The youngest children count the sheep and goats and search for animals that have wandered off. Two newborn goats are laid inside a large calabash that is lashed to a camel's back. The men and boys load their families' possessions onto the backs of the kneeling camels, ignoring their roars of protest.

Once the camels are loaded, they are lined up according to each family's importance in the **clan**. Each clan contains several factions, or groups, of between five and 1,000 people. Each faction is led by a headman, or elder. Now the people leave the patch of desert they have called home for the last seven days. They will walk until they find grasses for their herds. The journey might take them five miles or 50, one day or ten.

The Tuaregs glide gracefully across the sand dunes, their long flowing blue robes, called *boubous*, moving around them in the winds. By the time the first rays of sun appear, footprints are the only thing left to show where their camp has been. And a winter sandstorm will soon sweep even these away.

All across the Sahara, other bands of nomads are on the move. They follow the routes their grandmothers and grandfathers have taken before them, and their ancestors before them, in a line that goes back thousands of years.

Scenes like this one were once commonplace on the sands of the Sahara Desert. There was a time when the vast expanses of this desert, which occupies most of northern Africa, were home to many nomadic tribes, each with its own history, culture and language. Each tribe was like a movable nation, its members connected through their ancestors.

Today the number of nomads living in the Sahara is less than three million. Each year this number becomes smaller. Environmental problems have reduced the amount of grazing space, and the desert can no longer support so many people and animals. Also, many young people are lured away from the nomadic life by the growing urban areas in Africa, and they leave the hot sands of the desert for the easier life of the city.

But the Sahara Desert, and the people who live among its ever-shifting sand dunes and oases, are a fascinating part of Africa's history and its present. These desert dwellers are not citizens of any country. They have no passports, yet they roam across several countries. They are the citizens of 3.5 million square miles of shifting sand. By examining the lives of the nomads who have learned to live in this hostile region, we can learn not only about one of the central geographical areas of the African continent but also about a people and a way of life that have survived for centuries almost unchanged — a way of life which now faces a major turning point.

The Sailors of the Desert

Hundreds of years ago, the Tuaregs were pirates sailing a sea of sand. Their ships were their camels, and their targets were the camel caravans that crossed the Sahara laden with gold, ivory, sugar, tea and other riches. The Tuaregs would swoop down on these caravans, demanding a toll, or percentage of the goods the merchants were carrying. If the caravan leaders refused to pay, the Tuaregs would take what they considered their due by force. "Tranquility exists in the shade of sabers" is an ancient Tuareg saying.

Few people were able to withstand the might of the Tuaregs and their swift camels. Armed with spears, swords and daggers, the fierce warriors would charge into a caravan like a windstorm. The dark blue veils covering their heads prevented their victims from seeing their faces. Most traders gladly paid the Tuaregs their fee, happy to escape with their lives. As one Tuareg saying goes, "Who but a fool would dare seek vengeance in a land as foreign to him as the moon?"

The Tuaregs also raided the camps of other nomadic clans for food, animals and slaves. The Arabs to the north, Fulani to the south, and Moors to the west were all targets of Tuareg raids.

The only loyalty the people of the Sahara felt was to their clan. This devotion to family is just as strong today. If a cousin of a cousin of a cousin needs a sheep for milk or a place to stay, her clanspeople will give it to her. Not helping a relative, no matter how distantly related, brings shame upon the whole clan. "Give to your brother despite the fact that he has given nothing to you. God will give you whatever he does not give you back," one Tuareg proverb reads.

The Tuaregs say that they come from an island in the middle of the Atlantic Ocean. Over five thousand years ago their ancestors used to travel from the island to the Sahara. Back then, much of the Sahara was fertile grassland. Fishhooks and harpoons dug out of the sand are evidence of the shallow lakes that were once plentiful. Cave drawings in the area depict hippos, giraffes, crocodiles and other wildlife that could only have lived in a tropical climate.

Tuareg legend states that there came a time when the people tried to return to their homeland and found that the island had sunk into the Atlantic Ocean. They were forced to travel back to the Sahara and begin life there. In addition to the Tuaregs, there were the Moors, nomads who came from the country of Mauritania, and the Fulani, originally natives of Ethiopia.

Over the centuries, weather conditions in the Saharan paradise changed. The lakes evaporated and the grasses dried up. Strong winds swept away the topsoil, leaving only sand. **Desertification**, the changing of grasslands into desert, took its toll. Finally, all that was left of the fertile Sahara were small scattered islands of green, the *oases*, surrounded by a sea of burning sand.

The animals that once roamed the area migrated south to central Africa and beyond. But some species adapted to desert life, among them the gazelle, jackal, ostrich, giraffe, fox, scorpion and lizard.

Like the animals, the people also adapted. Some made the oases their home. But the nomads chose for their home the sweeping dunes of the desert. They lived by hunting, herding and raiding.

About 2,000 years ago the Romans invaded Africa and began the caravan routes across the Sahara. They hired the nomads to lead these caravans, which supplied them with food, treasures and slaves.

Then in the 11th century the Arabs invaded the Sahara — and stayed. They brought the Muslim religion with them and tried to convert the other nomadic tribes, using force when necessary. The largest group of Arabs came in 1045, when Egyptian Arabs, fleeing a famine in their homeland, migrated west. This added a fourth group of nomads, called the Arabic nomads. This group was composed of people from several different Arab countries.

Gradually, many of the other nomadic tribes converted to the Muslim religion. The city of Timbuktu located in what is now the country of Mali, became a holy city. No *nasrani*, or nonbeliever in Mohammed as the last prophet of Allah, was allowed to enter its gates. Timbuktu was the center for Islamic scholars until the 1500s, when nomadic warriors burned the city to the ground.

With several ethnic groups now competing for space, each group carved out different portions of the Sahara for its own. The Moors and Tuaregs claimed the salt mines of the west. Using slaves from other tribes, they excavated the salt and sold it. Because there was no way to refrigerate food, salt was used to preserve meat. It was also fed to animals to aid their diet. Once or twice a year, the nomadic overlords would journey the almost nine hundred miles to harvest their salt and supply the slaves that worked the mines with food and water to last them until the next time their masters chose to visit.

The Fulani chose the southern Sahara, where they remained herders, raising cattle to sell in central African countries. The Arabic nomads took the northern and eastern sections of the desert, which were closest to the countries from which they had come. They lived mainly as traders and herders.

Meanwhile, the camel caravans continued into the 1500s. Some trading caravans contained up to 10,000 camels. Laden with goods, they would travel to the Mediterranean and beyond. A caravan setting out from Timbuktu and heading toward central Africa might not return for eight months. Some never returned at all, falling victim to starvation, thirst or raids.

The nomadic peoples fought bitterly over territories, water, women, slaves and animals. It was impossible to unite the different groups, and often difficult to unite even the people of the same group. The Moors were so unwilling to accept authority that when the headmen of each clan held council to elect a new chief, the meetings often broke up into

fistfights. And a losing candidate's family, unhappy with the election results, might revolt against the new chief even before he left the election tent.

With the colonization of the Americas in the 1600s, the trans-Saharan trade fell off. Goods once obtained from the nomadic traders could now be bought more cheaply and easily from the new colonies. And slave traders, who once took their slaves up through the Sahara, now shipped their human cargo across the Atlantic from the Guinea coast rather than cross the desert.

Soon different European powers claimed parts of the Sahara as their own, although few Europeans actually settled in the region. Then in the late 1800s France, having lost most of its colonies to other countries, claimed the western Sahara as its own. The nomads, like the native Americans in the Americas, fought against the invaders. They said that no one owned the land, and that no one had a claim to it.

The French sent in soldiers to subdue the peoples. The nomads, particularly the Tuaregs, were enraged. The Tuareg leader sounded his *tobol*, or drum, calling the warriors to battle. In the end, it was not lack of courage that subdued the nomads, but their inability to unite. They could not put aside their tribal differences to fight their common enemy. Besides, camels and spears were no match against the French guns.

The fighting continued until 1917, when the rebellions ended. For many years after this, however, the French wisely did not travel through the Sahara unarmed or in small parties. They may have owned the land in name, but the oceans of the Sahara were still ruled by the roving pirates who had sailed its seas for centuries.

Today, the countries that make up the Sahara are independent from the foreign powers that once controlled them. But the nomads, who do not recognize any country's claim to the desert, still think of the Sahara as their own and do not answer to any government.

An Ocean of Sand

Examining the physical makeup of the Sahara helps in understanding just how remarkable the nomads are. Containing 3.5 million square miles of sand, the Sahara is the largest desert region in the world. The entire land mass of the United States would fit inside the Sahara's borders, with about 500,000 square miles left over. The desert covers the northern third of the African continent and includes within its grasp parts of Mauritania, Mali, Niger, Algeria, Libya, Chad, Egypt and Sudan. Morocco and Tunisia border it.

The Sahara stretches east from the Atlantic Ocean for 3,100 miles until it reaches the Red Sea. It runs south from the Atlas Mountains and the Mediterranean Sea for 1,200 miles before fading into the Sahel, which means shore. The Sahel is a strip of land, about 300 to 600 miles wide, that contains grasslands that nomads depend on for grazing land for their goats, sheep, donkeys, cattle and camels.

The popular image of the Sahara is one of a barren, desolate wasteland. Yet the Sahara is not one endless sea of sand — only 20 percent of it is. The majority of the desert contains mountains, high plateaus, towering rock formations sculpted by the wind, gravelly plains, and salt flats. And there are 800 square miles of oases to be found. An oasis is a fertile piece of land that grows around an underground spring. These can occur in the middle of vast stretches of sand, suddenly appearing as if out of nowhere.

The nomads of the Sahara are **pastoral**, which means that they depend mostly on their flocks of animals. To survive they need water and grasses for their animals. The animals in turn supply the people with meat and milk, from which they make butter, cheese and yogurt, the staples of their diet. They trade some of their livestock for grains, tea, sugar and other goods in markets that are held on the oases which are found throughout the desert.

In the Sahara, time is not measured by the hands of a clock. The desert's people live according to the seasons. The rainy season lasts from June until October. This is the time when the nomads follow the rains that bring the grasses. During the rainy season, the desert gets about three inches of rainfall. Temperatures reach a high of 130 degrees Fahrenheit, and you really can fry eggs in the sand. Once the sun sets, though, the desert cools way down. It is not uncommon for the temperature to drop 100 degrees at night.

When it does rain, often there is so little water that it evaporates before it soaks into the cracked earth. And sudden downpours can be deadly. *Wadis*, or dry river beds, spring to life as the waters rush from the highlands, sweeping away anything in their path.

The sandstorm, or winter, season lasts from October until June. It is a dry, dusty period during which the clans break into smaller groups and search for enough pasture to feed their herds. During this season, the nomads depend on water from wells. Some wells are simply holes

in the ground, others have been dug deep down into the earth. Some clans used to stretch goatskins across the tops of their wells, concealing them from strangers. This way, they protected their precious water supply. Thirsty travelers and traders whose caravans were out of water had to hire local citizens as guides.

Traveling this ocean of shifting sands and rocky terrain poses some difficult problems, and the nomads have developed different ways of dealing with their home. Each ethnic group travels in the same general area each year. They know by heart the landmarks and even individual sand dunes because they see them year after year, and their families have traveled the same paths for centuries. The best routes are handed down from one generation to the next like closely guarded secrets. This fixed pattern of migration is called **transhumance**.

If they travel at night, the nomads navigate by the stars. If they travel by day, they follow different landmarks. A nomad can tell where he is by the feel, color and even the taste of the sand or by the shape or number of hills in a certain area. Nomads seldom become lost, but their advice to fellow travelers is: "If you get lost, remain calm, for the desert is calm."

In the Ténéré, a great sandy region of the Sahara, a lone acacia tree was the only break in the landscape for hundreds of miles. The nomads used to navigate by it, and it was on all the maps. Then in 1973 a truck crashed into it, knocking it down. The tree was such a part of nomadic history that it was taken to a museum in Niger, and a monument was erected in its place.

The ancient trade routes that used to crisscross the Sahara have become the main roads for desert travel. They even have one route called the Trans-Saharan Highway. But highway, in the Sahara, means one-lane road. In the south, the highway is washed out by sand, and cars sink past their tire rims in its soft grip. Abandoned vehicles tell the stories of unfortunate travelers who got stuck and tried to walk to safety. In these areas, the most reliable form of transportation is still the camel.

The government of Niger has gone so far as to outlaw crossing the Sahara in certain parts with only one car. Tourists are urged not to travel at all during the scorching summer months. But people ignore the warnings, and each month the newspapers report the sad stories of

those who have tried to invade the nomads' unforgiving home and have been claimed by the desert.

Nomad children are taught the geography of their home through stories. Each black volcanic rock mountain with its peaks as white as snow has its own tale. For example, the 11,000-foot-high Tibesti Mountains contain hidden pools of water which are now used for washing clothes. Years ago, Tuareg warriors used these areas as bases for raids on unwanted intruders.

Travel is so rough across the sharp, black rock fields that caravans must move even more slowly than their usual two-mile-per-hour rate.

People driving land rovers over these bumpy plains have to change their tires two or more times on each trip because the sharp rocks slash the tires so easily.

Even more deadly than the rock fields are the **ergs**, which are great sand seas. With each step, a person sinks up to the ankles in the sand. No trees break the landscape. The Qattara Depression, which covers parts of Libya and Egypt, is always avoided. Its rippling sands are a breathtaking combination of pinks, browns, yellows, reds, blues and golds. But this beautiful ocean is really quicksand, and few living things can survive crossing it.

The sand dunes too are beautiful yet eerie. They can roll on in the same pattern for hundreds of miles. They are called live dunes, since they constantly shift position and shape. People can go to sleep near a dune and awake to an entirely different landscape.

The most deadly inhabitant of the desert is the **harmattan**, or sandstorm. Getting caught in one of these ferocious tempests can be deadly. Stories are told of thousands of animals and people becoming caught in the gale-force winds and being suffocated by sand.

The sandstorms occur during the dry winter season. They can be heard before they are seen, when an eerie moaning drowns out all other sounds. Then a pinkish brown cloud appears on the horizon, devouring the blue sky. Within minutes, a wall of sand envelops everything. The haze is so thick it blocks out the sun.

Once the storm is over, the people carefully shake the sand — inches of it — out of their belongings. They also shake out another deadly desert inhabitant: the large, green scorpion which hides in warm spots.

A favorite trick that the desert plays on those who try to cross it is the **mirage**. Often, travelers making their way across the searing sands suddenly think they see a lake, or trees, and get very excited. Racing to the beach, they find it is only another dune. Really, it is a mirage. A mirage is an image that is reflected on the layers of hot air that move over the desert. Acting as mirrors, these air waves can reflect the images of water that might be hundreds of miles away.

The hearts of the Sahara are the oases. Oases occur wherever water bubbles to the desert surface and creates a patch of vegetation. The

smallest ones support one or two families, while the largest have developed into small towns, centers of farming and trade. In the past, the oases were controlled by the nomads. Slaves and **Haratins**, black Africans from central Africa, were used to farm the oases. Haratin means one-fifth, which stands for the one-fifth of the crops that these people were allowed to keep from their farming. The rest went to the nomadic overlords, who in turn provided the farmers with animals, skins and other goods. Today, the oases attract peoples of many different cultures.

Most oasis towns look the same as they did hundreds of years ago. The houses are made of mud bricks the color of the sand. The streets are covered passageways just wide enough for donkeys and camels to pass through. Walking through them is like walking through a maze — it's dark and easy to get lost. Sand from the dunes surrounding the town drift into the houses and streets. The sand muffles all sound, and makes the oasis town unnaturally quiet.

During the afternoons, when it's hottest, most people gather outside, in the shade of the houses. Sometimes, at night, nomadic clans will come in from the desert and have parties or sing in the town's main square.

The oasis dwellers of the past would treat a visiting nomad group like royalty. They respected them for their ability to live in the harsh world of the desert, and welcomed the goods and news that the nomads brought with them.

The nomads looked down on the oasis dwellers because they were farmers. Nomads thought farming was the lowest form of work because it tied a person to one piece of land. But the nomads needed the crops that the farmers produced just as much as the farmers needed the nomads' animals and goods. It was a touchy interdependence. But without it, neither people would have survived.

The oasis farmer's main crop is dates — a staple of the nomadic diet. One date tree yields about 5,300 pounds of dates each year. And growing in the shade of the date palms are tomatoes, corn, grains and other vegetables. The Saharan peoples are experts at creating new date dishes, including date stew, bread and coffee. The leaves of the date palm are used for making rope, baskets, sandals, brooms, mats, hut walls and roofs, and ceremonial costumes. The wood is used for firewood and furniture. The date palm is so important, in fact, that nomads measure an oasis not by land size but by the number of trees it supports.

Water rights on an oasis are even more valuable than land. They are inherited, bought, sold and fought over. One person can own the land on an oasis and another person the water. Even one tree can have several owners.

In late summer, when the dates are harvested, the nomads return to their oases. In the past, up to 100,000 people gathered for these reunions. There is always a lot to celebrate — parties for all the marriages, births and birthdays that have occurred throughout the year. There are also weddings for the women and men who waited until

the reunion to marry. It is a happy time, and a once-a-year chance to see the whole family.

The people of the Sahara speak of their ancestral homeland with great respect and emotion. As something new happens, it is added to the oral history of the nomads. Parents share the stories of their ancestors with their children, so that events that happened long ago remain alive. These stories help to tie the people to the land and illustrate the folly of ever living anywhere else.

The desert is the people's teacher. It teaches patience and humility, generosity and trust. It offers the joy of awakening with the sunrise and living in harmony with nature. In the desert classroom, failure means death by starvation or thirst. However, where others have failed the tests, the nomads have not only survived but, for a time, prospered.

The Life of a Nomad

Within the four distinct nomadic groups, the people are divided into social classes based on lineage, language and job. In the Tuareg society, the largest of the nomadic groups, there are five distinct classes: nobles, vassals, craftspeople, farmers and slaves.

The nobles are the descendants of people who once ruled the nomads as kings and queens. Today, they are the leaders of the clans. The vassals are people who serve as the nobles' "knights," people who travel with the nobles but whose ancestors were not as mighty.

The third group, the craftspeople, are looked down on and feared by the nobles. They work with their hands, and the nobles fear their powers to make charms and work with fire. In the past, they acted as messengers and spies, camping beside the nobles' encampments. They traveled where their services were needed. Today, craftspeople make leather crafts and wooden utensils. They are also metalworkers, creating amulets and jewelry. Craftspeople are also the entertainers of the nomad tribes and often travel to different towns to perform.

The nomadic farmers, or Haratins, are looked down on by the other three classes because they are tied to a piece of land and are not free to roam. However, they produce most of the food needed by the other classes, so they are treated with respect.

The lowest class, the slaves, is composed mainly of black Africans kidnapped in raids. Traditionally, they cared for the nobles' animals, made the food, and performed other work. Up until the 20th century, slavery was common throughout Africa and the Middle East. Today, although it is against the law, some people still remain slaves. The people who own them call them "friends of the family."

Despite the great changes that have taken place in society, the nomads still hold tightly to their class system. While the nobles may not be kings and queens, they are still looked up to. While today's slaves may not be kidnapped from other tribes, they are still expected to work as hard as the captives of the past.

The life of a nomad changes very little over the years. The job each member of a clan holds is very well defined. Each person in the family knows what he or she is supposed to do, and children learn from their parents what is expected of them.

The day of a nomad woman begins at sunrise. Her husband, who is responsible for the herds, often brings her a bowl of fresh sheep's milk, which she shares with her children. The woman is responsible for making all the food, including butter, yogurt and cheese. She also grinds grain between two rocks until she has powder. From this, she makes *couscous*, a ricelike dish.

It is also the woman's job to make and dye clothes, weave the baskets that store the food and cradle the babies, and cut and braid the hair of her family. Girls begin helping their mothers as soon as they are able to hold a stick to stir the couscous.

Women in nomadic society are highly respected. Among the Tuaregs, women hold property, have a choice about their marriage, and take part in decisions about family and clan matters. Indeed, it is not unusual for a woman to own more sheep, goats or camels than her husband.

A nomad man's day begins before sunrise, when he goes out to tend to his herds. After feeding and milking the animals, he goes back to the tent for breakfast. He spends the rest of the day herding the animals, **bartering** with other nomads, and teaching his children the ways of the desert. At night, he may talk over clan business with other nomads or join in a round of storytelling and singing with the rest of the group.

The tent is the center of a nomadic encampment. Within a tent's walls, business is conducted and everyday life is lived. Each nomadic group has its own distinct type of tent. The Fulani use mainly round grass tents, which take an hour or so to set up and are easy to break down when it is time to move.

Moor tents are made of black goat-hair blankets. The tent is divided down the middle; one side is for the women, the other for the men. The women own the tents. If a Moor woman leaves her husband, she packs up her tent and returns with it to her parent's clan.

The Arabic nomads use large blanket-tents that date back to biblical times. Inside the tents are low bed-couches and carpets. The cooking area is to the left of the entrance. If an Arabic nomad man has more than one wife, he must provide each one with a separate tent.

"If ever our hearts are to be close together, then our tents must be far apart," say the Tuaregs. Like the other nomadic groups, the Tuaregs greatly respect privacy. They have camel-skin or woven grass tents. Fringes of leather in the Tuareg colors — green, red and blue — dangle from the tent roofs. Their food is stored in tripods, hung in calabashes in trees, or kept in separate tents.

Eventually, there comes a time when a clan has to move. "We depend on God and camels," says Ali, a Moor headman living in Mauritania. His parents, wife and two children, sister and brother-in-law, two brothers, and two cousins and their families all travel together as a clan. Ali has many camels, which means he is rich and respected.

Camels are so important to the peoples of the Sahara that there are dozens of words for them. The name that an owner calls his camel can indicate its sex, age, health, color, quality, defects and behavior. For example, in the Tuareg language, an *arennenas* is a male camel who neighs happily when he sees something that gives him pleasure.

The desert and camels were made for each other. This sturdy animal can go for up to 12 days without water. It has long legs, so its body is four feet above the earth's surface, where the air is 40 degrees cooler. The camel's woolly hide acts much like a nomad's boubou; it keeps heat out and body moisture in.

Most of the camel's body fat is located in its hump. The camel can lose up to one-third of its body weight without harm. Camels who have lost 227 pounds after eight days with no water can gulp down 27 gallons at one sitting and gain all of that weight back.

Each day, Ali gives his five-year-old son Ahoudan lessons about the desert, camels, and other things necessary to make him a good nomad. The boy is already an expert shepherd. Ali watches as his son sketches in the sand brands, or marks of ownership, of other nomads' camels. Ahoudan must learn about 3,000 different brands and be able to identify the tracks of at least 1,000 individual camels.

Just by looking at a camel's tracks, Ali can tell the beast's sex, owner and how long ago it passed by. He easily picks out his own camels' prints from thousands of other tracks.

At clan reunions and other celebrations, the men race their camels. The Tuaregs have traditionally had the fastest camels. They also dance their camels, often under the light of the moon. While the women play drums and sing, the men move their camels to the rhythm, performing intricate patterns.

The camel that dances and races is white. It is a more graceful, more sensitive and finer boned animal than its brother, the brown

baggage camel used for caravans. It also has great endurance, and is able to travel 400 miles in six days.

But even the fastest of camels must stop to eat, and the fastest of cameleers, people who herd and ride the camels, must stop to sleep. The nomadic encampments are the hotels of the desert. When a group of weary camels and their drivers has no camp of their own, they will seek shelter at a camp along their path. Hospitality in this hostile land is expected, even if the "guest" is an enemy. This is one of the strongest unwritten laws among the different nomadic groups.

When a traveler reins in his camel outside an encampment, he waits for the clan elder to come out. Women and children peer out from the openings of their tents and watch as the elder advances and shouts, "His peace be with you."

"Peace be to you," the stranger responds.

"No evil," says the elder, and the traveler repeats the same. They will then ask each other about their families, their herds, their tents, and their ancestors, all the while thanking Allah for His blessings. With each greeting, each tries to figure out what sort of person the other is.

Even if all of a clan's animals have died, its people are sick, and its tents have been lost in a sandstorm, the elder will not say so. These things are considered Inshallah, or the will of Allah. It is believed that complaining about Inshallah will bring bad luck, for who is to guess the purpose of Allah, the creator of the world.

Once inside the camp, the guest is taken to the headman's tent. There he is given three cups of green tea. This drinking ceremony is practiced by all the nomadic tribes. Traditionally, the tea is brewed by the men or by a servant. The first cup is strong, to cut the harsh taste of the desert sands. The second is very sweet, to give love. The third and last, the weakest, adds pleasure. The Saharan people drink tea often, as much as three or four times each day.

In some camps, girls might hide during a stranger's visit, thinking that he has come to marry one of them. If a young woman's clan is doing badly, she might be given in marriage to a guest in exchange for a flock of sheep. This "bride price" might be necessary for her clan to survive, but it makes for some very unhappy brides. Thankfully, this practice is becoming a thing of the past.

When a camp has sheep or goats to spare, and often even if it doesn't, one is slaughtered for dinner to honor the traveler. In one Fulani clan, the visitors are served all of the meat. It is then up to them to share it with their hosts. When the guests leave, they are given the sheep's skin, heads, hooves and tail. These things prove how generous the hosts are, and travelers are expected to share this news with everyone they meet on their journey.

Nomads practice the Muslim religion, following the teachings of the prophet Mohammed and their holy book, the Koran. Even their religion has been adapted to suit the desert. The veils traditionally worn by Muslim women as a symbol of modesty are not worn in the desert. And the **mosques**, or churches, so important in the cities, are nonexistent in the desert. The nomads' mosques are wherever they set up their altars to pray to Allah.

The **marabouts** are the holy men of the nomads. They are respected, feared, and sought after for advice. They send people on journeys with Allah's blessings. In return, the people provide them with food and shelter.

The marabouts also make good-luck charms, or amulets, for their followers. Most nomads have silver boxes or leather pouches dangling from their necks or waists. Inside are verses from the Koran that relate to what the person asks of Allah. These wishes may include protection from sickness or enemies, the desire for a wife or husband, or a request for an easy journey.

At the end of the rainy season, in late September, the clans have reunions, at which the members of a tribe join together to celebrate a successful year. The Fulani unite for cattle drives into central Africa. Boys five or younger go with their fathers on these trips, working right alongside the men. They learn the cattle business from their fathers, who sell the cattle in Nigeria for up to $400 a head. In a land where most people don't make more than $500 a year, many Fulani have become rich.

During these drives, women and girls travel in the opposite direction of the men, moving north, deeper into the Sahara. They will set up camps and, when the trading is over, the families will be reunited.

The pattern of nomadic life is unchanging. The clans move as their herds need new grazing lands, when it is time to harvest the dates from an oasis, when it is time to sell their cattle, or when it is time to make another trip to their salt mines. Just as the moon moves through its different phases, the nomads travel in an endless cycle begun thousands of years ago.

The Nomads Today

In the early 20th century, the automobile was introduced to the Sahara. Camel caravans, which could only travel at about two miles per hour at their quickest, were replaced by much faster trucks.

The nomadic tribes turned to herding exclusively, having given up trading, raiding and slaving. Where once the Tuareg women sang of great warriors, they now sing of the men with the best herds. The only wars fought were over women, and the weapons were romantic poems and songs. To display their skills as camel riders, Tuareg men began to perform intricate camel dances.

In 1948 the French built the first of many deep wells around the pastoral zones in the south. Anyone with a rope, bucket and pulley could use them free of charge. Before, permission had to be granted from a well's owner. In 1964 French engineers installed gasoline pumps in the wells so that they drew water automatically. The long, tedious process of watering flocks by hand was shortened drastically.

Many clans changed their traditional migration routes and began to camp near these wells for the entire length of the dry season. Traditional wells fell into disrepair. A tribe's herds no longer had to be spread out; they grazed around the gasoline-powered wells.

The rains were so good that the farmers began working the land further into the Sahel, the border of the Sahara. They did not rotate their crops, however, and were planting cash crops like peanuts that were exported for money but which also depleted the soil and left it useless.

To many outsiders, it seemed as if the nomads and the farmers were thriving. In fact, the two groups were on the edge of disaster and about to fall over — and it all had to do with rain.

In 1968 the rains did not come. That year, many nomads lost up to 50 percent of their herds. "It is the will of Allah," most nomads said about the disaster. After all, there had been droughts before. No one dreamed that this drought would last for seven years, until 1974.

The pasture surrounding the gasoline-driven wells was quickly overgrazed and eroded. Sand replaced the grass. The nomads were forced to choose between watching their herds die of thirst or of starvation. And as their animals were dying, so was their way of life.

The people begged their marabouts for help. But no verse from the Koran could protect people from drought. Families split up as men tried to find work, walking hundreds of miles to cities. Refugee camps sprang up outside most cities and oasis towns. People sold everything they had just to get to the camps, where they were given a small amount of food and water.

From Mali to the Sudan, the people were starving, and their governments didn't have the resources to help them. When help from other countries did come, it was too late. The countries most affected were not able to get the food to the people quickly enough. There weren't even enough trucks to transport it. People starved in camps while grain piled up in warehouses.

Under this strain, the social life of the nomads fell apart. The workers and slaves of each ethnic group left them to forage for food. Workers in the refugee camps said that many Tuaregs died not of starvation, but of sadness for the loss of their way of life.

One Tuareg noble hitched a ride into Niamey, in Niger. He was hired as a house guard. When he had worked for several months, he sent his wife money to join him. The new family "camp" was the courtyard of his employer's house.

When the rains did begin to fall again, the people danced under the cloudy skies, their arms outstretched to the heavens. The rains, though, could not replace the herds lost by the Fulani, Tuaregs, Moors and Arabs. Many nomads remained in the refugee camps because they had nowhere else to go. The desert that they had served all of their lives had turned its back on them. Today, they live on the outskirts of cities and have become beggars.

In 1991 a reporter traveling with a salt caravan through the Sahara asked its Tuareg leader if he was a rich man. The Tuareg said no.

"Who among you is rich?" the reporter asked.

"There are no rich Tuaregs," the cameleer replied. "The drought made them all equally poor."

The silence that followed the man's words was more disturbing than the stillness of the desert.

Yet the nomads survive. They control the salt-caravan trade because only their camels can pass through the great sand seas surrounding the mines. Besides, the profit made from the salt trade is so small that they are the only ones left who think that it's worth the trouble.

Many nomads also make money by guiding tourists across the Sahara. But some of those who have lost their herds have also lost their dignity. Encampments have sprung up alongside main roads. Whenever a truck stops, children and adults appear from out of the dunes, begging for water, sugar or tea.

A new way of life has evolved for some nomads in which one family member goes off and works in a city for several months, returning for three months during the harvest time. During the dry season, clans take their herds right into the cities, where there is water. The livestock feed off of the garbage.

Many areas of the Sahara are still overgrazed almost 20 years later. The governments simply do not have the money needed to bring back to life land that the desert has claimed. The result is that even the towns

are beginning to be engulfed by sand dunes. The more this happens, the more vulnerable the people are to being devastated by drought again.

The Saharan countries are among the poorest in the world. Most have gained independence from foreign control only since 1960. As a result, their governments are unstable, concerned mainly with controlling civil wars and preventing military overthrows, which happen in Africa with alarming frequency. One thing does, unfortunately, remain stable in these countries: they don't want nomads wandering across their lands.

The problem is really one of conflicting lifestyles. The nomadic way of life is based on the idea that no one owns the desert, and that each tribe works for its own good. Government officials have no tolerance for a way of life that doesn't work for the majority of society, that doesn't pay taxes, and that smuggles goods across borders. It doesn't matter to them that the nomads have little money and are simply trying to preserve a way of life that has existed for thousands of years.

The governments have also caused the breakup of the nomads' way of life by outlawing nomadic schools and forcing children to leave their families to study in town schools. While the parents see that their children are becoming educated, they also see their society vanishing, as no one is left to help on the farms or travel with the herds. Governments refuse to help, because they want the nomads to stop wandering and settle in one place.

Pressure also comes from within the nomadic tribes. As more young people go to schools in the cities, they see just how hard life in the desert can be. Many are choosing not to return, settling for the relatively easy life of city dwelling. Also, like any wild creatures, the nomads are disappearing as their habitat disappears. Forced to adapt to a life in one place, they no longer are the rulers of the desert, and their mighty deeds are becoming no more than stories told around camp fires.

In Mauritania, where the president is the son of a nomad, the situation is not as bad. There the government digs new wells when old ones run dry. Yet even there, the nomads are becoming sedentary. In 1960, when Mauritania gained independence, 80 percent of the people were nomads. By 1985 the percentage had dropped to 25 percent. And it continues to drop.

As the north African countries develop their resources, industrialize their economies, and educate their people, the wanderers are forced to give up their dreams. In many places, the nomads can no longer buy what they need with animals — money has replaced the barter system.

The recent discovery of oil in the north has also brought changes to the Sahara. Oil rigs are taking the places of oases, and many nomads have taken work on them. Libya and Algeria have become oil rich. Tunisia is also exporting oil, but has had trouble drilling in its shifting

sand dunes. The money made from oil has helped the governments of the north improve the lives of the sedentary population, but not the lives of the wandering nomads.

An accidental bonus of the search for oil was when drillers discovered **aquifers**, huge pools of water, from 300 to 6,000 feet below the surface of the desert. In Libya these pools are being pumped to the surface and used to turn the desert into farmland. The danger is that this water source can never be replenished. Once the water is used up, no more will replace it. Then the farmlands that they are being used to create will dry up and become part of the desert once again.

The Future

The Sahara and its people are at a crossroads. Not quite a part of Middle Eastern culture like most Muslim areas, the Sahara is also not quite a part of black Africa. However, its people are inextricably bound up in the same struggles that face the rest of Africa. The nomads have shown repeatedly their remarkable ability to adapt to life under the harshest conditions nature can throw at them. But now they must face even harsher conditions, those imposed by governments that don't see the need to preserve the nomadic lifestyle and by a society that is slowly surrounding them and forcing them to change.

Perhaps the key to survival lies in the teachings of the desert. The nomads have learned humility, respect and great love for their home. They have gained strength and bravery. If they remember their lessons, despite the changing ways, then maybe they can not only survive, but prosper throughout the remainder of this century and beyond.

PHOTO IDENTIFICATION

(Cover) A young Tuareg with his family's camels in Timbukto\Mali; (**4**) a Tuareg woman at a clan gathering\Algeria; (**6**) veiled women of the Requibet tribe\Algeria; (**8**) a nomad guard on patrol\Algeria; (**10**) desertification in the Sahel\Niger; (**13**) cattle search for grazing land in the desert\Mauritania; (**14**) Berbers\Algeria; (**16**) sand dunes\Algeria; (**19**) a donkey-powered well\Algeria; (**21**) the Trans-Saharan highway\Algeria; (**23**) the oasis of Taghit\Algeria; (**25**) women collecting dates on an oasis farm\Chad; (**26**) a young Tuareg\Mali; (**29**) a slave girl of the Tuaregs pounds grain\Algeria; (**31**) a nomadic encampment\Mali; (**32**) feeding the camels\Algeria; (**34**) a Fulani cattle market\Morocco; (**36**) a Tuareg mounted on a white camel, the breed for which nomads are famed\Algeria; (**38**) desertification\Algeria; (**41**) a clan sets out\Algeria; (**43**) nomad women\Algeria; (**44**) reclaiming land lost to desertification\Niger; (**46**) a Tuareg man\Niger

Glossary

Aquifer A body of water found 300 – 6,000 feet below the surface of the desert.

Bartering A system of trading goods and services for other goods and services without using money.

Caravan A group of nomads who travel together.

Clan A group of people who are related by either blood or common ancestry.

Desertification The process of turning an area into desert by destroying the vegetation.

Erg A vast expanse of shifting sand.

Haratins A group of nomadic blacks from central Africa who are often employed by Saharan nomads to farm oases.

Harmattan A fierce desert storm that creates huge clouds of sand.

Marabout A nomadic holy man, similar to a priest.

Mirage An optical illusion caused when layers of heated air reflect the image of something very far away and make it appear close by.

Mosque An Islamic church.

Nomads The name given to the different people who live in the Sahara Desert and have no fixed homes, but travel from place to place with their flocks in search of grazing land and water. The nomads are made up primarily of the Tuaregs, Fulani, Moors, and Arabic Nomads.

Oasis A body of water found in the desert around which a settlement develops.

Pastoral A word used to describe a society that is centered around farming and caring for livestock, usually sheep, goats, or cattle.

Transhumance The fixed migratory routes used by the nomads which are handed down from generation to generation.

Index